Of Magic Sails

Of Magic Sails

A photographic history of air travel, 1926-1976

ISBN: 0-915174-02-2

Library of Congress Catalog Card Number: 75-36369

Printed in the United States of America

Written, designed and produced by Graphic Alliance, Inc. Chicago, Illinois
Research and Text: Barbara Bean
Design: C. A. Islinger

To all air travelers, in sincere appreciation of their loyalty,

enthusiasm, and support. Without them,

a great industry would have remained a vision,

precluding "all the wonder that would be."

Contents

Preface

For I dipt into the future, far as human eye could see,
Saw the vision of the world, and all the wonder that would be;
Saw the heavens fill with commerce, argosies of magic sails,
Pilots of the purple twilight, dropping down with costly bales.

—Alfred Lord Tennyson, *Locksley Hall*, 1842

More than a century ago, Alfred Lord Tennyson had an astonishing view of the future, a vision of *magic sails* that would fill the skies. In his mind's eye, he saw the day when airplanes would span the globe, creating new bonds among the peoples of the world.

On December 17, 1903, at Kitty Hawk, North Carolina, Tennyson's dream moved toward reality, with the 12-second, 120-foot flight of the Wright brothers. Inspired by their accomplishment, men and women throughout America labored to translate poetry into fact. Determined and daring entrepreneurs, engineers, pilots, government officials, and a host of other visionaries slowly advanced the art and science of flight.

By 1926, air transportation was a reality. Congress looked forward to turning over the Post Office air mail routes to private airline operators, hoping that soon they would carry not only mail, but passengers.

Although air transportation had advanced, it still took a touch of imagination to believe that much would come of the infant industry. It took men who were willing to gamble on a risky proposition—men such as Walter Varney, a former California flying-school and air-taxi operator, and one of his instructors, Leon Cuddeback. They decided to bid on the air mail route between Elko, Nevada, and Pasco, Washington, via Boise, Idaho, despite discouraging reports about the riskiness of the proposed route.

Varney and Cuddeback drove by car over the terrain and discovered that the worst reports were accurate. Between Elko and Boise were great stretches of desert and broken volcanic hills that would make an emergency landing extremely risky. From Boise north, the route passed over a short stretch of level farm fields that ended abruptly in badlands, leading almost to the foot of the Blue Mountains of Oregon, subject to severe winter storms. Wheat fields blanketed the north slopes of the range for many miles before the fairly level approach into Pasco.

Others who surveyed the proposed route dropped out of the bidding. But Varney and Cuddeback were determined to get that route and fly it. They would fly it in single-engined, open-cockpit planes. They would fly it without the benefit of light beacons, radio-direction beacons, two-way radios, or weather reporting service. And they would do it all with only one accountant, a traffic manager, four pilots, four mechanics, and six Swallow planes.

But Varney and Cuddeback were not the only dreamers in the Pacific Northwest. The citizens of Pasco and Boise shared a dream of magic sails that would someday carry them to faraway places. In the sullen light of dawn on April 6, 1926, 2,500 spectators gathered at a recently cleared field on the outskirts of Pasco. Visitors had come from as far away as Seattle to witness the inaugural flight of Varney Air Lines.

At 6:23 A.M., after fussing with a balky engine, Cuddeback took off on his historic flight. His cargo was 9,825 pieces of mail, weighing almost 200 pounds, mostly stamp collectors' first flight letters. He flew through torrential rains and thunderstorms, squinting through the wind screen while rain lashed his face and ran down his neck.

A few minutes past 10 A.M., the small gray Swallow appeared through the mist at Boise. Cuddeback made a perfect three-point contact with the yellow sands of the runway and came to a stop halfway down the field. Turning sharply, his plane threw up sand, spraying youngsters who ran in the plane's wake.

"I'm for a big beefsteak and long nap after I reach Elko," Cuddeback told the reporters and officials who swarmed around as he stepped out of the plane. He was handed two mail sacks to carry to Elko, along with a bag of prize Idaho potatoes destined for President Calvin Coolidge. As the citizens of Boise celebrated the occasion with a parade, Cuddeback flew on to Elko without incident. The challenge had been met.

Fifty years later, small Varney Air Lines had long since become part of United Airlines, and instead of a few lonely, open-cockpit airplanes droning along the first airways across America, there are the heavens filled "with commerce, argosies of magic sails" foreseen by Tennyson.

Foreword

Over the past 50 years, air travelers have witnessed and participated in dramatic changes and tremendous growth in the U.S. commercial aviation industry. The payload once was strictly mail; today it is chiefly passengers. The equipment once was single-engine propeller planes; today it is multi-engined jet aircraft. The scope of service once was a few passengers; today the airlines dominate intercity mass transit.

While the public has watched the airlines grow, the industry has watched the passengers and seen them change. In the early days, it took an adventuresome soul to climb into a plane and fly under generally adverse conditions.

But the steady maturing of the industry over five decades has made the experience of flight so routine for many travelers that the aircraft is less the end than the means—a connecting link between one office and another, or between a home and an ocean beach many miles distant.

Thanks to the support of millions of loyal passengers over the years, the air transport industry in the United States celebrates its golden anniversary in 1976.

The privately owned U.S. airlines operate more than 2,000 modern aircraft, which knit together 58,000 city-pairs in the world's finest air-transport network. More than 200 million passengers annually rely on the nation's domestic airlines to carry them safely, quickly, and comfortably.

The airlines have become potent forces fostering economic growth. They have accelerated the movement of goods throughout the land, and established themselves as an essential part of the American business community. Less well known is the important role of the airlines in national defense, providing transport in times of emergency and flying peaceful missions for the government.

Tourist attractions have blossomed because jetliners—scheduled and chartered—carry large numbers of people quickly and economically. The hotel and auto rental industries have widened their business vistas, corresponding with airline growth. Today's extensive professional sports schedules rely on the services of commercial aviation. The air carriers are major employers; last year, about 300,000 people earned their livelihood in the U.S. airline industry.

With the possible exception of electronics, no other U.S. industry born so late in the twentieth century has progressed so rapidly to become a pivot point of commerce and a familiar part of the lives of millions of people.

Many could argue about the group to which air transportation is most indebted for its impressive achievements. Certainly the pioneers contributed much, as have others down through the years. Shareholders, banks, and insurance companies played vital roles. Manufacturers provided the necessary technology and equipment. The federal government furnished useful guidance and assistance.

In United Airlines' view, however, the main incentive for improving our service and broadening our operations has been the customer. Without the encouragement and support of air travelers over the years, the progress of this industry would have been severely limited. We believe it fitting, therefore, to dedicate *Of Magic Sails* to all air travelers.

Edward E. Carlson
Chairman and Chief Executive Officer,
UAL, Inc., and United Airlines

1926–1930

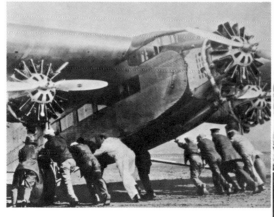

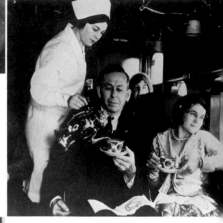

"One day the air mail pilots dropped in at the ice house, I met them, and said, 'Won't it be wonderful when they can take passengers.'

"'Oh, we take passengers now. We have two extra cockpits.'

"I said, 'No kidding?'...and so I just decided to fly."

—Maude Campbell
Western Air Express'
first woman passenger,
Salt Lake City–Los Angeles

Maude Campbell was one of about two thousand Americans who in 1926 "just decided to fly" with the air mail. Clinging to hard wooden seats in open-cockpit planes, often half buried by mail bags, and outfitted in flying suits, leather helmets, goggles, and parachutes as their only protection against the elements and the vagaries of flight, these first passengers received little encouragement.

The pioneer airline operators were primarily concerned with carrying the mail, for which they received subsidies from the federal government. In 1926, the Post Office turned over its air mail "feeder" routes to private airlines, retaining the main transcontinental route for another year. On April 6, 1926, Varney Air Lines inaugurated service between Pasco, Washington, and Elko, Nevada via Boise, Idaho. Varney in 1931 became part of the United Airlines system, along with three other pioneer air mail operators, Pacific Air Transport, Boeing Air Transport, and National Air Transport. On April 17, 1926, Western Air Express, which later became Western Airlines, initiated service between Los Angeles and Salt Lake City. Throughout 1926, routes were taken over by a number of other airlines that were to form the nucleus of the country's commercial aviation system. Companies like American Airlines, Eastern Air Lines, Northwest Orient Airlines, Pan American World Airways, and Trans World Airlines also trace their origins to pioneer air mail carriers.

To these first airline operators, passengers took up valuable space and caused a great deal more trouble than a mail bag. They expected to arrive on time for their appointments, got thirsty and hungry and cold and airsick. They even expected pilots to serve as tour guides. The tiny airplane engines then available could not power a big enough plane to carry passengers and the full load of mail, so most airlines tolerated passengers only when the mail load was light.

Oh, are you going too?

Travelers often eagerly arrived at the airfield, only to be greeted with a rueful stare and, "Oh, are you going too?" Once airborne, many a passenger must have wondered himself. "Comfortable" was not the adjective to describe open-cockpit flying.

One passenger hurrying to the National Air Races reported that he flew "perched on top of the mail, clinging to a strut or whatever was handy, to avoid being bumped off when we ran into rough weather. I arrived at my destination greatly resembling the tar baby, having been right behind a leaky oil pipe on the way down. The first person I met at the races...remarked, 'It sure beats hell how dirty the trains are getting.'"

In 1926, the pilot was his own dispatcher; he interpreted weather reports and plotted his route with a compass and a road map. Often he wandered off course to investigate a fire or landed to chat with another pilot. This independence led to some problems. One pilot was unaware that his compass was being deflected 150 degrees by a load of metal. Departing from New York, he turned left at what he thought must be Lake Erie. Actually, it was the Atlantic Ocean. Flying aimlessly around New England, looking for Ohio, he finally ran out of gas, landed, and dragged a Connecticut farmer out of bed. "Where's Cleveland?" the pilot demanded. Still half asleep, the farmer answered, "Cleveland's dead. Hoover's the president now."

Passengers become popular

Things could only get better. Gradually, the airline operators saw that Americans really did want to fly. They realized that if they could build bigger planes, they could make extra money from passenger travel and supplement the air mail subsidies. As engine manufacturers developed more powerful engines, aircraft manufacturers in turn built larger, more reliable aircraft.

San Francisco to New York – 1927					
Plane	Cruising Speed	Number of Passengers	Time	Fare	Number of Stops
Boeing 40–A	105 m.p.h.	2	32½ hours	$404	15
Curtiss Carrier Pigeon	120 m.p.h.	1			

Services: San Francisco to Chicago—a box lunch and thermos of coffee, Chicago to New York—a thermos of cold water

Total passengers carried by scheduled domestic airlines, 1927: 9,000

The trickle of passengers swelled dramatically after Charles Lindbergh flew the Atlantic in May, 1927. Americans decided if Lindy could brave the ocean, they could surely risk a short air trip. Even more important, the flight brought big money to airlines that had previously struggled along with only the government's support. Aviation stocks became the biggest sellers on the exchange, and Wall Street financiers bought controlling interest in the more successful airlines, thereby furnishing the money needed to buy better equipment and improve passenger services.

One of the first airlines to go after the passenger market was Boeing Air Transport (BAT), an arm of Boeing Airplane Company. Boeing bid on and won the western segment of the transcontinental route when the Post Office turned it over to private operators in 1927. BAT flew between San Francisco and Chicago with 40–As, which had room for two passengers who crammed into a miniscule cabin between the wings.

And a free box lunch to boot

Arthur M. East, of New York, described his 1927 trip in a Boeing 40–A, a 24-hour flight that left San Francisco at 7:20 A.M. and arrived at Chicago at 7:05 A.M. the next day:

"The cabin is about the size of an ordinary railroad Pullman seat with room for two persons, entirely enclosed with not more than six inches of head room...." At the first stop, the passengers "crawled out of the cabin and down off the wings by means of a ladder, the wings being about five feet above the ground...." After several more stops and several box lunches provided by the airline, the weary East grumbled, "They again furnished us with a box lunch and somehow we felt they were trying to rub it in.... They also gave us a fresh thermos bottle."

At Cheyenne, Wyoming, the passengers suddenly noticed that the pilot "had a funny package strapped across his back and upon learning that it was a parachute, we immediately made a request that we also be provided with a parachute. This rather amused the Boeing Transport officials, but they said they would see we were outfitted at North Platte."

By the late 1920s, passenger service was becoming more sophisticated and more comfortable. Transcontinental Air Transport's air/rail service spanned the continent between New York and Los Angeles, serving meals off "Diri-gold" plates. Western Air Express received a $180,000 loan from the Guggenheim Fund for the Promotion of Aeronautics to experiment with new services for passengers in luxurious Fokker planes. Boeing built the trimotored 80–A. Its cabin had mahogany paneling, leather upholstered seats, and hot and cold running water. Meals were served by nurses hired to tend to passengers' needs. These young women were called "stewardesses."

The cabins were still small and confining by today's standards. Air sickness was common, as the planes churned through the rough weather, not around or over it.

Few passengers of today, however, experience the thrill and wonder of flying that enthralled America's first air travelers. As Sacramento passenger Ralph Clark sighed, "It was with a touch of regret that we clambered out of the plane. The flight was over. We were mere mortals walking upon the earth again."

In the Roaring Twenties, everyone was adventurous. Americans lost their hearts to a brave, bashful, young pilot named Lindbergh; dashing movie heroes risked their celluloid lives to save fair, young maidens; people stealthily knocked at a speakeasy door and whispered, "Joe sent me." And when it ended with the 1929 Crash—all the glitter, all the wealth, all the illusions—people milled aimlessly through Wall Street, dazed and disbelieving.

Going, going, gone. And ticket number one on America's first commercial airline was won by A. C. Phiel with his bid of $400. Subsequent passengers, foregoing the honor of being first, paid only $5 for a ride on the Benoist seaplane that shuttled across Tampa Bay during the winter of 1914, shutting down after only 2½ months. On January 1, 1914, the *Tampa Times* covered the first flight: The pilot "rose to about 150 feet so as to give his passengers a better view of the city, which must have been a wonderful one indeed. He can go even higher if he chooses."

A passenger peers out of the improvised cabin in this Ryan Airline plane (lower left), which flew passengers between Los Angeles and San Diego in 1925. Although short-lived, the airline surprised everyone by showing a profit in its one and only year of operation—then the owners decided to concentrate on building airplanes rather than flying them.

Seeing the few attempts at founding airlines fail, Congress authorized the U.S. Post Office to support the development of air transportation; they started in 1918 to fly the mail in converted World War I fighter planes like this de Havilland DH–2.

A typically courageous Post Office pilot was Jack Knight, the jaunty young man below the propeller at right. Knight rescued a dramatic San Francisco–New York, day-and-night flight from failure. Flying from Cheyenne, Wyoming, he arrived in Omaha, Nebraska, only to discover that his relief pilot had failed to show. Knight volunteered to continue to Chicago, a route he had never flown. Enthusiastic farmers and chamber of commerce members lit bonfires to guide him. The 1921 flight slashed cross-country flying time in half, to 33½ hours, and helped convince Congress to appropriate $1.25 million to expand air mail service and light the airways.

With the new funds, the Post Office set up beacon lights and laid out emergency landing strips along the transcontinental route (left). Nervous farmers were reassured when pilots told them that having a beacon on their barn was an advantage, because pilots flew a half mile to the right of the beacon.

An enthusiastic crowd of 2,500 lined the runway to witness the takeoff of the inaugural flight of Varney Air Lines, from Pasco, Washington, to Elko, Nevada, on April 6, 1926.

Spectators crowded around the plane of Lieutenant Oakley G. Kelly, flight commander at Pearson field, Vancouver, British Columbia, who arrived with four escort planes from Portland, Oregon, and the postmaster of that city to salute the Varney flight (right).

A federal marshal guards the loading of the mail on a National Air Transport plane. In 1927, NAT was awarded the New York–Chicago leg of the transcontinental route, and despite the importance of this route, it actively discouraged passengers for several years. The rugged individuals who managed the entire cross-country trip paid $404 for the 32½-hour flight with 15 stops. They were offered several box lunches between San Francisco and Chicago and a thermos of cold water for the trip to New York.

"Passengers were greeted with all the enthusiasm reserved for a carrier of bubonic plague, and the pilots took great pains to discourage such would-be adventurers. After all, they reasoned, why put up with some hare-brained fool who would get sick at the least little maneuver, when it was really Uncle Sam's mail that paid the wages."

—J.H. "Slim" Carmichael
pilot, later president of Capital Airlines

In open-cockpit days, passengers were often weighed along with the mail. This fellow may have taken a tip from veteran pilot Ham Lee, who often smoked "the biggest, blackest cigar I could buy. In cold weather I thought a cigar kept my nose warm and melted the frost from my eyelashes."

Pilot Fred Kelly wing-wagged to signal fellow Western Air Express pilot Jimmy James to land in a field so he could meet Kelly's famous passenger, movie star Bebe Daniels (far right).

Her flying suit disguising her fashionable plus fours and gold Mary Jane-style shoes, Maude Campbell poses for photographers with Western Air Express president Harry Hanshue (lower right). The girlfriend she was visiting worked at the gas company on Flower Street in Los Angeles. The girl and her fellow employees were "hanging out of the window all afternoon waiting for this tiny plane; of course, there weren't any planes flying around then. When I got there, they were all excited…anybody flying…wondered how I had the nerve…but knowing me, I always was adventurous."

Boeing Air Transport, Western Air Express, and Western Electric cooperated to develop a two-way radio-telephone for aircraft, which some pilots grumbled would only lead to the guys on the ground telling them how to fly.

Some airlines experimented with enclosed-cabin planes. If you think you would suffer claustrophobia from being squeezed into a toothpaste tube with the mailbags, consider the poor passenger braving a Minnesota snowstorm in an open-cockpit plane, thoughtfully equipped with skis.

Weather was a critical factor, and pilots eagerly scanned weather reports at each stop. The January, 1929, issue of Western Air Express' *Dashboard Record* told of a flight that encountered bad weather and was forced down atop a mountain in Utah in subzero weather. The pilot hitchhiked to a farmhouse and telephoned Salt Lake City for help. A rescue truck was sent, but it couldn't get within a quarter mile of the Fokker F–10. Pilot and passengers helped carry 1,100 pounds of mail and their baggage to the truck, then headed for the nearest town, pushing the truck uphill and riding downhill.

Stout Air Services, operating between Detroit and Grand Rapids in 1926, originated many passenger services. The seemingly blase passengers at left, accompanied by a uniformed "flight escort," may just be dazed. One early Ford Trimotor passenger was an engineer who later helped develop the DC-1. He recalled: "The thing vibrated so much it shook the eye glasses right off your nose. In order to talk with the guy across the aisle, you had to shout at the top of your lungs...the...wicker...chairs were about as comfortable as lawn furniture, and they were so narrow they pinched your fanny. When the plane landed on a puddle-splotched runway, a spray of mud, sucked in by the cabin air vents, splattered everybody!"

—Douglas J. Ingells
The Plane That Changed the World, A Biography of the DC-3

Ford Airport in Dearborn, Michigan, included a modern terminal with wicker chairs, fireplace and an esplanade for watching planes. The country's first airport hotel was just across the street.

The Ford Trimotor, (right) designed by William B. Stout, was one of the most popular planes ever built. Watching it waddle down a runway, its corrugated aluminum skin rattling enthusiastically, it was easy to see how it came by its nickname, "The Tin Goose."

17

Airports were often nothing more than a hangar, a few beacons, and a dirt runway. Some progressive airlines provided a passenger terminal with a few chairs, a board listing flights, and a ticket counter. Passengers had their baggage weighed outside near the plane, and sometimes found themselves helping push the plane into position for takeoff. By 1928, airlines had downtown ticket offices in major cities, like this Pan American office in Miami.

The dedication of a new airport was an important event. The opening of the Burbank, California, terminal was celebrated with demonstrations of flying skill as impressive in 1928 as the Blue Angels' performance today.

In 1925, Charles Lindbergh was an unknown air mail pilot flying for Robertson Aircraft Corporation in St. Louis, Missouri (upper right).

On May 20, 1927, he made his bid for the $25,000 prize offered by Raymond Orteig, a wealthy Frenchman, for the first nonstop airplane flight between New York and Paris.

Taking off in a Ryan monoplane named "The Spirit of St. Louis," the handsome young pilot disappeared in the gray mist; a light rain was falling. Americans sat by their radios during the hours of silence waiting for news of the plane, which carried no radio and no parachute. Finally, word came that Lindbergh had been sighted off Ireland. After a 33½-hour flight, he touched down at LeBourget airfield outside Paris. Cheering wildly, thousands of onlookers mobbed him as he climbed out of the tiny plane.

Their whistles blasting, boats crowded around the government cutter carrying Lindbergh and President Calvin Coolidge to a New York ticker-tape parade and reception in Lindbergh's honor.

One of the favorite air trips for pleasure-loving Californians was the short hop by seaplane to Catalina Island (far left). The route was operated for several years by Western Air Express, which advertised itself as "the world's shortest overseas airline."

Boeing Air Transport began flying between San Francisco and Chicago in July, 1927, with the Boeing 40-A mail plane (upper left). Chicagoan Merrill C. Meigs, the six-foot four-inch publisher of the *Herald Examiner*, recalled years later, "In spite of 10 stops which enabled us to stretch a few minutes, it was several days before I loosened up the kinks...Oh, my aching back!" The slightly larger, more powerful 40-B had room for four passengers (lower left).

In 1929, the Boeing 80 (right) was introduced; it carried 12 travelers in comparative luxury. Passengers could check the cabin clock and working altimeter or follow the sights out of the window with the help of an air log furnished by the airline.

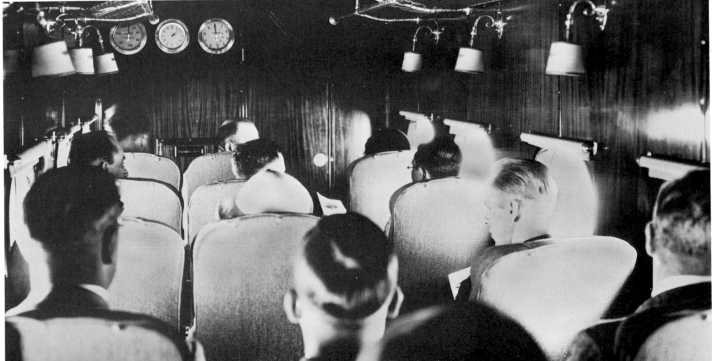

Will Rogers (right) helped to popularize air travel. In his newspaper column, magazine articles, and radio programs, he enthusiastically described his frequent flights around the country, convincing many people to fly. In an article in the January 21, 1928, *Saturday Evening Post*, he told about the box lunches furnished by the airline at each stop: "Well, all this eating is mighty fine, but it has its drawbacks. The more he [the fellow next to him] ate, the more he expanded...I have killed a whole ham and six chickens, an armful of pies and cakes and a clothes basket full of odds and ends and haven't got to Omaha yet...I could never make a long distance flight; they couldn't carry enough grub to keep me."

In 1928, the Guggenheim Fund for the Promotion of Aeronautics loaned Western Air Express $180,000 to operate a "model airway" between Los Angeles and San Francisco. Passengers were flown in luxurious Fokker F-10 trimotors, featuring mahogany paneling, a completely appointed lavatory, and individual reading lights. Other amenities included flight attendants, sandwiches, a free limousine ride to the airport, and a complimentary birchwood parchment air log. A *Los Angeles Times* cartoon called this service "the very newest wrinkle."

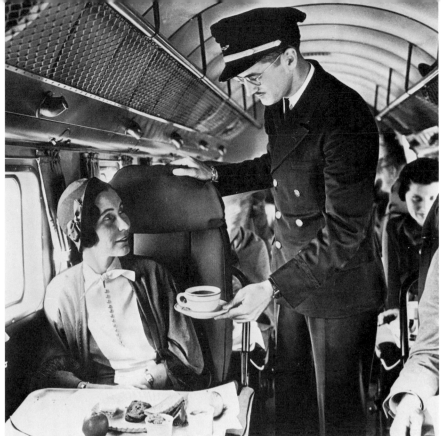

In 1929, Transcontinental Air Transport, a predecessor of TWA, and the Pennsylvania and Santa Fe railroads cooperated in coast-to-coast, air-rail passenger service. TAT flew passengers by day in Ford Trimotors, transferring them at night to Pullman cars.

The total trip took 48½ hours and cost $339.98. Service was deluxe, with meals being served off Diri-gold tableware on lavender tablecloths. Speedy Aero-Cars transported passengers between train and plane.

Passenger Walton Forstall, a Philadelphia engineer, reported, "Flying as we did…gave a wonderful opportunity to 'see the world go by.' And what an interesting world it was…It had not yet grown used to our tremendous three-motored Ford. The roar of our propellers brought humans to look up and wave, dogs to bark defiance, made horses and cattle scamper wildly, and drove chickens to the nearest cover, seeking refuge from some gigantic hawk."

Shown here are the Winslow, Arizona, airstation (left) and the Columbus, Ohio, station (below), where passengers are boarding a plane for the July 8, 1929, inaugural flight, after arriving on the overnight train from New York.

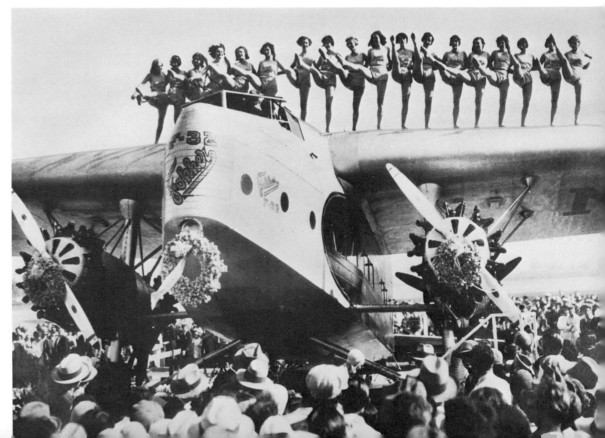

Cushions were stuffed with rubber balls, so passengers would feel they were "riding on air" in the four-engined Fokker F–32, which carried 32 passengers in eight lavishly decorated compartments (left). At Western Air Express inaugural ceremonies in 1930, the Fanchon and Marco chorus line danced on the wings of the huge airplane.

Inflight radio entertainment was not a new idea when it was reintroduced in the 1960s. Northwest Airways, a predecessor of Northwest Orient, equipped its planes with radio receivers and individual headphones in 1929.

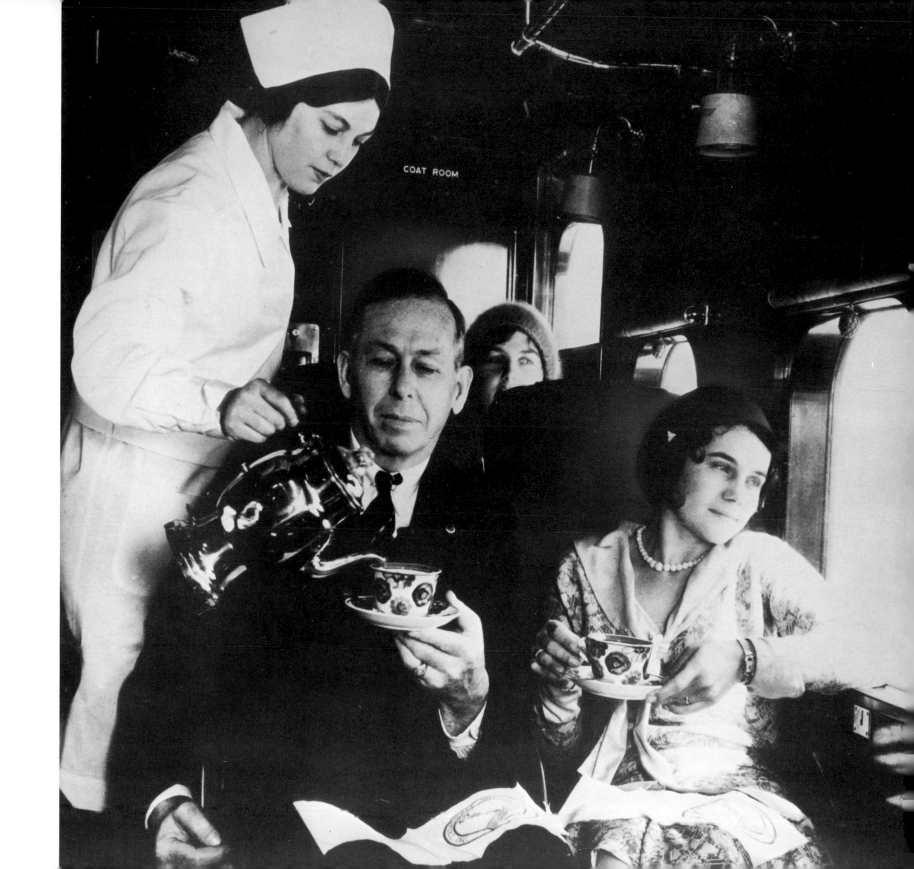

In 1930, Boeing Air Transport division traffic agent Steve Stimpson suggested that the airline hire young women as "couriers."

"Imagine the psychology of having young women as regular members of the crew," he wrote to Assistant to the President William A. Patterson, who later became president of United Airlines. "I'm not suggesting at all the flapper type."

In an article in the May 15, 1970, *New York Times*, one of the first stewardesses, Inez Keller Fuite, recalled, "We had to carry…luggage on board. And if the seats weren't fastened down tightly, we had to bolt them down ourselves.

"Some of us had to join bucket brigades to help fuel the airplanes. We also helped…push planes into hangars. And we had to make sure that the passengers didn't open the exit door by mistake when they were going to the washroom."

Stewardesses dispensed cold chicken, apples, rolls, and cake from picnic hampers and poured hot coffee from thermos bottles. The first stewardess wardrobe was a starched nurses' uniform, a dark green, double-breasted jacket and shirt of jersey, and a green tam. A flowing cape was added to protect the stewardess against chilly airplane cabins and drafty airports.

The Boeing Monomail, introduced in 1930, employed a radical new design. The streamlined, all-metal monoplane gave air travelers a glimpse of the sleek planes to come.

1931-1941

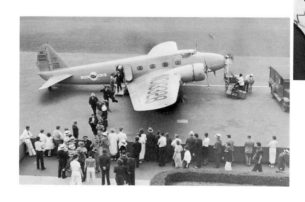

"The DC-3—now there was a plane! Oh, you had to walk uphill to get to your seat, and it was tiny by today's standards, and it plowed right through the worst weather, but you couldn't help love her."

—Ken Case
buyer from New York City

Despite the advances made in the late 1920s, air travel in 1931 was still an unpredictable adventure. Schedules were erratic, and airplanes carried passengers in varying degrees of comfort and speed at altitudes where turbulent weather often occurred. Passengers could never be sure they would not end up hiking or riding a farmer's truck to town and continuing their trip by train. More often than not, a trip by air was prompted either by a desperate attempt to reach the bedside of a dying relative or by a sense of adventure, a desire just to "see what it's like." It was not a dependable form of transportation.

During the Depression, one airline went so far as to require its employees to ride along on almost-empty flights, dressed in civilian garb, so air travel would appear to the few nervous passengers as slightly more popular than the facts indicated. In 1935, only 675,000 Americans—half of 1 percent of the entire population—had ever flown.

Behind the scenes, things were improving. In 1930, Congress passed the McNary-Watres amendment to the Air Mail Act, which changed the airlines' subsidy from payment per pound of mail to payment for space, no matter whether the planes were filled with mail, cargo, or passengers. The airlines immediately started shopping for larger airplanes.

The first "modern" airplane was the Boeing 247, which began service in 1933. A low-wing, all-metal monoplane, the 247 carried ten passengers at 155 m.p.h. United Airlines bought the new planes and cut cross-country flying time to 19½ hours, half of what it had been with the Boeing 80-As.

TWA, suddenly at a severe disadvantage with plodding Ford Trimotors, put out bids for a competitive airplane. Douglas Aircraft Company responded with the DC-1, a twin-engine monoplane with such innovations as wing flaps and variable

pitch propellers. Like the 247, it had landing gear that retracted into the belly of the plane to streamline its flight. In three days of test runs in 1934, the prototype broke three and set eight American speed records.

The airplane that was eventually sold to the airlines was redesigned to incorporate the new, more powerful Curtiss-Wright Cyclone engines. This DC-2 could carry 14 passengers at 155 m.p.h, and it was the first plane with the range to fly around the most severe weather.

Knight in shining armor

Meanwhile, American Airlines, the third transcontinental line, was losing money with its uneconomical Curtiss Condors, the nation's first sleeper planes. The company asked Douglas to develop a slightly larger version of the DC-2, one that could accommodate berths for cross-country overnight flights. The resulting Douglas Sleeper Transport (DST), introduced in 1935, had 14 berths. The day version, with 21 seats, was the famous DC-3. A stubby, all-metal plane, the DC-3 was fast and uniformly dependable, often performing above and beyond the call of duty. With a cruising speed of 180 m.p.h, it cut the nonstop flying time between Chicago and New York to four hours. It carried twice as many passengers and double the amount of cargo and baggage as the Boeing 247, now only two years old and already obsolete.

Ralph Martin, a veteran Cincinnati air traveler, recalls his travels on the DC-3: "At the time, we all thought it was the ultimate in travel…and it was. But, looking back now, I have to laugh. It was so small, and in rough weather almost everybody was air sick. It jerked through the skies like a bucking bronco. It took about 15 hours to fly across country, with three or more stops. But it was a real improvement then. Who knew what was coming?"

San Francisco to New York – 1937					
Plane	Cruising Speed	Number of Passengers	Time	Fare	Number of Stops
DC-3	180 m.p.h.	21	15½ hours	$160	3

Services: Pre-cooked meals reheated in plane's galley, overnight sleeper planes with Pullman-style berths, stewardess service
Total passengers carried by domestic scheduled airlines, 1937: 981,000

Americans had been impressed in 1932 when for the first time a presidential candidate flew with his family to accept his party's nomination. It was on this nine-hour flight from Albany, New York, to Chicago that Franklin Delano Roosevelt put the finishing touches on his acceptance speech, adding a significant line: "I pledge myself to a New Deal for the American people."

A few years later, it was commonplace for important political figures and celebrities to travel by air. Corporation presidents wrote articles in business publications explaining why it made sense for salesmen and executives to fly. Airline publicists saw to it that photographs of Hollywood celebrities boarding airplanes appeared regularly in newspapers. And in 1939, the Green Bay Packers became the first pro football team to charter an airplane to fly to a game.

O promise me

With larger airplanes to fill, the airlines courted the traveling public vigorously. United Airlines' aggressive sales department sent letters and folders describing the airline's service to every person who registered for a Reno divorce. Or, you could choose the Reno marriage package: a ten-minute ceremony complete with license and flowers, a lively rendition of "O Promise Me," a hotel room, breakfast, and round-trip transportation for two between San Francisco and Reno—all for the regular price of one round-trip ticket bought by the groom. The company reported a brisk business.

'Way back then, United had a "take-me-along" campaign, too: Wives were given free passes when they accompanied their husbands on trips. The airlines learned a few lessons from this campaign. Scribners of September, 1938, reported that as one plane was loading, "a taxi careened through the barrier and pulled up by the plane. Out got a large lady who dived into the cabin and came out leading an elderly man by the ear—much to the chagrin of a long slim blonde,

sheepishly following in his wake." Depite a few such incidents, the campaign ended successfully, and the airline sent letters to the wives, thanking them for accepting the offer. Unfortunately, a few wives didn't remember going!

Aloha by air

In 1936, Pan American, which had been testing ocean flight in the Caribbean since 1927, began passenger service from San Francisco across the Pacific, stopping at Honolulu, Midway, Wake, and Guam before landing at Manila—a trip that took six days. By the beginning of World War II, Pan American had also inaugurated service from Seattle to Alaska and across the Atlantic to Spain. The world was shrinking fast.

In 1941, almost 4 million Americans, 3 percent, had flown, and new challenges were met. In 1940, Boeing developed an aircraft in which cabin air pressure was controlled to stay at sea level or slightly above, regardless of the aircraft's altitude. Planes with pressurized cabins could carry passengers comfortably to 20,000 feet, above much of the worst weather. TWA ordered five of the new Stratoliners, but within a year, these planes and the newly developed DC-4s were flying a different kind of passenger and a different cargo—military personnel and weapons to fight a world war. Not until after the war did passengers have a chance to fly in pressurized planes, and by then, more advanced aircraft like the DC-6 and the Constellation were available.

This was the age of heroes—the great Babe Ruth kept belting them out of the park, Franklin Delano Roosevelt promised a New Deal to lead American out of the Depression. Through the magic medium of radio, people were inspired by the president's fireside chats and cheered by comedians like George Burns and Gracie Allen. And at the movies, they escaped from hard times with Shirley Temple.

Celebrities took to the air in the 1930s, and the airlines made sure that photographers were on hand to snap their pictures—hoping to convince the rest of America that one didn't have to be crazy to fly. After all, everyone was flying—Fred Astaire and his wife Polly, Eleanor Roosevelt, the Andrews Sisters, Ozzie and Harriet, and those inimitable Marx Brothers…well, being crazy didn't hurt.

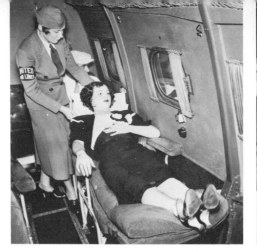

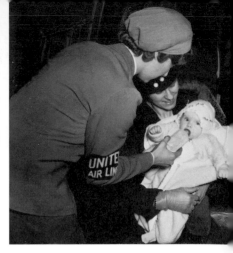

As airplanes became more sophisticated, so did onboard entertainment. Passengers received election bulletins during the 1932 election on United Airlines flights (left center), and in that same year, Western Air Express gave an airborne demonstration of a new invention—television (lower right). Stewardesses carried baby kits for infants.

The first modern airliner, the Boeing 247 (lower left), was introduced in 1933. Navigating its narrow aisle and clambering over the wing spar that cut the cabin in half was no mean feat (upper right). As one passenger reported in the December 3, 1933, *Toledo Sunday Times*, "My first feeling of real awe and admiration for the sky stewardess came early in the trip when I decided to move from the front seat of the plane to one in the rear. The weather was rough and the huge Boeing was swaying and lunging. [The stewardess] progressed nimbly down the aisle. In a pathetic though noble attempt to follow her I came in very personal contact with each of the seven other passengers, stumbling to the right and falling to the left."

On November 8, 1934, thousands of
New Yorkers turned out to witness the
first arrival of Eastern Air Lines' "Florida
Flyer," a spanking new DC-2 (upper
right). The larger, faster DC-3 (left),
introduced a year later, was the most
popular plane ever to fly the skies. By
1939, it was carrying 90 percent of
civilian air traffic.

Stewardesses could hold their jobs only
as long as they remained single, which
usually was not long. In 1936, one airline
encouraged its sky girls to pledge, "I will
not leap in Leap Year."

The airline industry's first flight kitchen was opened by United Airlines in 1936 in Oakland, California, enabling the airline to serve a wider variety of hot meals. Closed forever was the "fried chicken era" that a lot of old-timers like retired Chicago executive Tom Jamison remember: "I traveled almost every week on business in the thirties, and I got so I'd dread the moment I was face to face with another fried chicken. I still hate it…"

Passengers on the overnight DC-3 sleeper planes (right) traveled in style—breakfast in bed and then off to the spacious lounge to change while a steward made up the berths. Upper berths folded into the ceiling, while lower berths were transformed into two facing seats. By day, meals were served on tables that hooked on the walls, complete with crisp white linen, fine china, and bouquets of flowers.

As air travel became more commonplace, improved terminals catered to passengers' needs and comforts on the ground. One airline traffic manager, Gertrude Mason, provided this explanation for improvements in airport facilities: "A man may not grumble if he finds the airport has a shanty for a depot and that he must wade through inches of dust and gravel to get to the plane—but such a condition will give any woman a ground for complaint." Denver's airport (lower left) boasted a modern terminal, but a dusty field.

Although Newark terminal (right) may have been impressive to the local chamber of commerce, one Chicago reporter grumbled in 1933, "New York is the goal, not the mangy-looking airport." Coming back home to Chicago's Municipal Airport (upper left), he seemed more impressed: "The Lindbergh beacon is sighted and then the glaring Wrigley building. The ship banks and turns; the flood lights of the Municipal Airport throw out a blanket of shimmering silver light across the field."

Reservations in the 1930s could be handled by a simple merry-go-round system; four reservation clerks and dispatchers answered phones, checked schedules for flights, and marked off reservations on nearby control boards.

In December, 1932, four airlines set up their own traffic control centers at Newark airport to coordinate the increasing traffic. By 1938, there were 11 such centers at the country's busiest airports, managed by the newly formed Civil Aeronautics Administration.

Chicago reporters were not the only ones to complain about Newark's airport. New York Mayor Fiorello LaGuardia (right) refused to leave a plane that landed at Newark, insisting, "I bought a ticket to New York, not New Jersey, and I expect to be taken to New York." Shortly thereafter, he pushed for the construction of a New York City airport, which was opened in 1939 and was named after him (bottom right). Only a 25-minute drive from the New York business district, the new airport was a showcase facility, with a landscaped park along Long Island Sound and a three-story terminal (center right) with restaurant, bar, barber shop, florist, haberdashery, jewelry shop, beauty salon, brokerage office, and post office. Passengers could easily reach the airport by limousine from Central City Terminal (top right), which was across from Grand Central Station. The city terminal also provided many services for airline passengers, including a 600-seat newsreel theater.

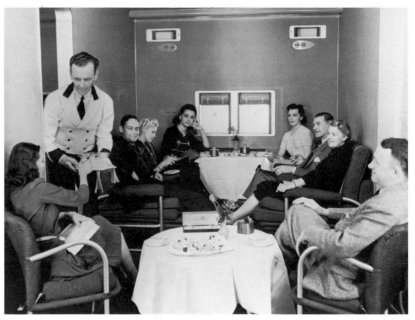

"Eleven men and two women will eat hot bouillon, chicken fricassee with potatoes, boiled beets, lettuce and tomato salad, French pastry, tea, coffee or hot chocolate more than 500 miles out over the Pacific this evening—and while they're dining, they'll be making history."

On October 21, 1936, this dramatic paragraph in the *San Francisco News* reported the first transpacific passenger flight from San Francisco to Manila, via Hawaii. It was a 14-hour overnight flight to Honolulu, Hawaii, and passengers paid $360 for a one-way fare to the Pearl City airbase (top left). Those first passengers flew in a Martin M–130, which had seats for up to 32 passengers and ample room to stroll around.

By 1941, the larger, even more luxurious seaplane, the Boeing 314, (shown over the Golden Gate Bridge), was spanning not only the Pacific but also the Atlantic. This "ocean liner of the skies" had seven large compartments (bottom left) resembling drawing rooms, with straight walls and a flat ceiling—even a private "honeymoon suite" in the rear. Rested and relaxed, passengers debarked in Hawaii after an overnight flight.

1942-1957

"Before the war, we just didn't take airplanes that seriously. But World War II changed all that. And, when the war ended, I remember I wanted to enjoy things, and I really wanted to fly."

—Ted Bennett
insurance executive from Los Angeles, California

Would-be airline passengers during World War II did not get very far without the password: priority. At the onset of war, the airlines had converted half their fleets to military use. In 1939, they had 378 airplanes to carry almost 2 million passengers; in 1943, midway into World War II, the airlines had only 165 planes left for domestic service, yet they carried 3.5 million passengers.

Since only one in three persons who requested a seat could be accommodated, the airlines set up a priority system, consisting of four grades that were based on the value of the trip to the war effort. Ordinary travelers had to take a chance on getting a standby seat, knowing that even when they got one, they stood a good chance of getting bumped by a priority passenger at the next stop. One Los Angeles reporter, assigned by his newspaper to cover a story on the East Coast, flew coast-to-coast in a surprisingly swift 44 hours. His return trip took nine days.

Meanwhile, the military half of the airline fleet, stripped of passenger comforts and painted drab olive, was ferrying military personnel and equipment around the world under contracts with the Air Transport Command (ATC) and the Naval Air Transport Services (NATS). The airlines had only 14 planes and the military only 12 planes capable of overseas flight at the beginning of the war. By the end of the war, ATC had 3,000 aircraft, and domestic airlines on military missions were stretching their wings to China, Africa, Australia, and South America. In many places, the airlines had to establish ground-navigation facilities, airports, and weather stations. With pilots and other male employees in military service, women filled many jobs formerly held by men: engineers, traffic managers, control tower operators, pilots, and aircraft factory workers. "Rosie the Riveter" became a patriotic symbol of the national war effort. Airline employees also volunteered to sell war bonds in their spare time, and airplanes were painted with patriotic slogans such as "Victory in the Air."

Travel boom

Americans endured the curtailment of air travel during wartime, but as soon as restrictions were lifted, they flooded the airports, with money to spend and eager to pursue the ordinary pleasures that were denied them during the war. The airlines were almost overwhelmed by the rush of passengers. They were still trying to reconvert military aircraft to civilian use and retrain employees returning from the service. Airports built to accommodate a few hundred passengers a day were suddenly handling thousands. In August, 1946, an issue of *Fortune* lamented: "The beauty and wonder are about the only compensation for airline travel in 1946. To travel by plane, a passenger must now sacrifice his comfort, his sleep and often his baggage."

Eager to capture this vastly expanded travel market, the airlines bounced back. By 1948, they had quadrupled the size of their fleets. New four-engine airplanes carried passengers in unparalleled comfort and at record speeds: DC-4s, DC-6s, doubled-decked Stratocruisers, and Lockheed Constellations. In 1953, the DC-7, the first plane that could fly nonstop coast to coast, cut the flying time to seven and one-half hours.

San Francisco to New York – 1950					
Plane	Cruising Speed	Number of Passengers	Time	Fare	Number of Stops
DC–6	300 m.p.h.	56	9½ hours	$158	3

Services: Complete hot meals, coach and family discount fares, complimentary cocktails, lounges
Total passengers carried by scheduled domestic airlines, 1950: 17,468,000

Babies and bacardis

The industry's introduction of coach fares in 1948 was soon followed by discount fares for families. The postwar baby boom hit the airways, and kids were given free balloons and "wings"; stewardesses distributed baby kits complete with food, diapers, and talcum powder. Adults received extras too. Northwest Orient Airlines began to serve liquor in its Stratocruiser lower-deck lounges, a move that involved numerous legal tangles. States below Northwest's routes granted (or refused to grant, in the case of New York and Illinois) aerial liquor licenses. Westbound passengers could order drinks after takeoff from Newark, New Jersey, and unless the weather was bad, and the plane was diverted over New York, liquor was available until the plane reached Illinois. Then things got confusing, as the October 7, 1950, issue of *The New Yorker* described them: "Wisconsin, Minnesota, South Dakota, North Dakota, Montana and Idaho are all wet except on Sundays and Election Days. Over South Dakota, it is illegal to serve a spendthrift, but Northwest hasn't yet challenged a passenger under this statute. Washington, like Michigan, has a three percent sales tax. In order that a lounge steward may know what state he is in or over, and thus what laws are momentarily in effect, the pilot keeps in touch with him by means of the intercom." One can imagine the poor passengers, with drinks yanked from their hands as the invisible border was passed.

Ground down

Things may have been getting rosier in the sky, but on the ground, bottlenecks remained. Reservationists had trouble keeping up with the ever-growing number of calls. Ticketing was still completed tediously by hand, although carbon-paper tickets did replace the long string of tickets for interline flights. The airlines also saved time by eliminating the passenger manifest, which required that each passenger check in with one ticket agent. Now, passengers could check in at any of several counters. United Airlines developed the first self-claim baggage service, helping to shorten the time needed to claim one's luggage. Airports were still antiquated and undersized for the heavier traffic, however. Jets, with greater passenger capacity and speed, were coming soon, promising to complicate things even more.

At the beginning of the war, only 3 percent of the population had ever flown. At the dawn of the jet age, in 1957, 15 percent had flown, and America was on the verge of an explosion in air travel. It was becoming the most popular form of mass transportation, edging out trains and buses. Between 1947 and 1957, the airlines boosted their share of all intercity traffic from 9 to 40 percent. And the boom was just beginning.

Whether standing in line for a sugar ration card or fighting in the front lines, every American did his or her part to win the war. And when it was over, everyone celebrated—welcoming back General Eisenhower and the fighting men and women—and then turned back to the pursuit of happiness—cheering the Yankees on to another pennant or taking a long-overdue vacation.

Americans were proud and confident, and they basked in the glamor and glitter of Hollywood, the familiarity of radio and television stars, the human side of flinty Harry Truman, and Ike's broad smile. Nostalgic for the good old days? Test your memory of these stars of the forties, shown here on the inaugural flight of TWA's "Star of California" Constellation in 1946.

During World War II, commercial pilots flew military supplies around the world. One Western Airlines pilot, quoted in *Western's World* magazine, told how he made it from Fairbanks to Anchorage, Alaska: "You just put your ship into a steep climb as soon as you take off. You don't level off until your props are churning stardust. Then you hope you're at a spot in the Alaskan mountain range where Mt. McKinley ain't."

An air traveler with the enviable priority rode in DC–3s, stripped of berths to make more room for all the passengers who wanted to fly. Without a priority, it was another story: "Twice I pleaded for mercy. I was told there might be a seat on the next flight. Each time I was called back just as I started for the ramp. The last time was about 3 A.M. I had not slept for 45 hours. My face felt like dirty sandpaper. My suit was fetchingly pressed in horizontal creases. My voice, when I tried it, sounded like something out of a jar of rusty nails."

—Don Eddy
The American Magazine
February, 1945

At its Cheyenne modification base, United updated more than 5,000 Flying Fortresses fresh out of aircraft factories, to keep them apace with the fast-changing military technology. Lessons learned in combat were quickly translated into improved fighting equipment aboard these planes.

Victory was the outcome, thanks in part to wartime activities of airline employees like former United Airlines stewardess Ellen Church, (second from left), who was awarded the Air Medal for her service as a flight nurse. Stewardess Mary O'Connor (third from left) organized and directed the navy's air evacuation school. At war's end, the airlines struggled to retrain employees returning from service, while facing a flood of travelers.

A reason for the big swing to air transportation in the 1950s was the impressive performance of the airlines during the war and technological advancements that made air travel safer and more dependable. Radar, for example, was developed during World War II and later led to an improved system that could bounce echoes off storm clouds 100 miles ahead so airplanes could detour around them.

Everybody was in a hurry, in a hurry to get ahead, in a hurry to have a good time. And that meant going by air. Passengers came in all sizes—babies, children, grandparents, even the family pet. And it seems that in the confusion, many people left something behind, usually their hat, which ended up in the airline's lost and found.

Air travelers found new comforts aloft, including pressurized cabins. Postwar aircraft were much roomier and quieter than earlier airlines. Despite these advancements, some problems remained:

"You learned how to balance on those airplane rides in the forties, trying to eat off a tray that perched precariously on a pillow in your lap. If you hit an air pocket, well, forget it. Once, I remember, we hit one just as the stewardess was bending over to hand me a coffee cup. The plane dropped, she went with it, but the coffee just stayed there, suspended for one awful second—then sploosh! all over me."

—Fred Daniels
salesman from Houston, Texas

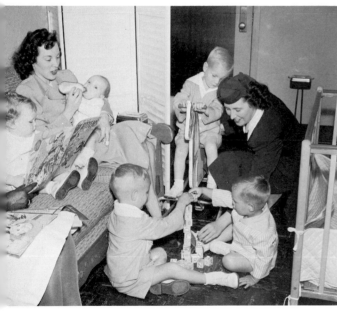

Airline reservation agents using hand-set availability boards were swamped, and often it took eight to ten calls to get a confirmation. New methods were devised, including machines that electronically queried master control boards. In 1958, the first modern computer system kept a running inventory of reservations, cutting manual operations by half and reducing time by as much as 75 percent.

Meanwhile, airport terminals built for prewar travel markets became inadequate to handle the passenger boom. Washington, D.C.'s National Airport terminal (upper left) was jammed, and Denver's airport terminal looked old-fashioned next to the modern airliners of the postwar period. In August, 1946, *Fortune* wrote of the problem: The Chicago airport "is the worst. . . .At almost all hours every telephone booth is filled, with people lined up outside; the dingy airport cafe is filled, with standees. To rest the thousands, there are exactly twenty-eight broken-down leather seats. One must line up even for the rest rooms. . . .The traveler consigned to hours of tedious waiting can only clear a spot on the floor and sit on his baggage and, while over-smoking, drearily contemplate his sins."

As the decade progressed, the new four-engine aircraft cut flying time to a fraction of what it had been during the war. One of the most popular planes was the doubled-decked Stratocruiser, with a cruising speed of 300 m.p.h., a capacity of 50 to 100 passengers, and sleeping berths for overnight trips. Leisurely flights to Hawaii allowed time for sipping champagne, enjoying elaborate multi-course meals, or having a cocktail in the lower-deck lounge.

Airlines christened the luxurious DC–7 in the mid–1950s. The world's fastest piston-powered transport, it had four powerful Curtiss Wright engines that delivered 13,000 horsepower at takeoff. The DC–7 cruised at 365 m.p.h. and was the first airliner to fly nonstop coast-to-coast schedules.

Sleeper planes were on the way out, since few flights were long enough to allow time to make up berths. TWA's Super Constellation featured "Siesta" seats, which extended fully for comfortable napping. First-class passengers were served complimentary cocktails and hors d'oeuvres in the lounge.

Several airlines introduced turboprop planes such as the British-made Viscount, which first flew commercially in 1955. These airplanes, powered by jet engines that drove propellers, were soon surpassed, however, as the 1960s approached.

Nobody was embarrassed to be a male chauvinist in 1955; nobody even knew what one was. Informal "Men-Only Executive" flights (lower far right) pampered businessmen, cushioning their ride with cocktails and cigars.

1958-1967

"I'm leavin' on a jet plane,
Don't know when I'll be back again . . ."

"Leavin' on a Jet Plane"
by John Denver

On December 10, 1958, National Airlines introduced the first domestic jet service by flying a Boeing 707 between New York and Miami. The 120-passenger plane cruised at almost 600 m.p.h., 6 to 8 miles above the ground. By 1960, Americans could reach any place in the continental United States within six hours flying time.

The jet age was here. Now, no jet airport on the globe was more than a day away from any other jet airport. Americans secretly, and not so secretly, dreamed of taking off on a jet plane. . .to the Rockies for a ski weekend, to California for sun and surf, to a balmy holiday in Honolulu, even to a theater weekend in London.

Surveys made the year before the first jet was introduced showed that 72 percent of Americans who had flown wanted to ride in a jet. And, as it turned out, once they flew in a swift, smooth, quiet jet, they did not want to fly in anything else. Airlines that had planned to switch their prop planes to shorter routes discovered that passengers grumbled. New short-to-medium-range jets were ordered—Caravelles, Boeing 727s and 737s, and DC–9s.

For the 62 percent of the American population who had never flown, it was a different story, and it was these people the airlines needed to attract to fill the jets, which were twice as big as prop planes. They wooed first-time passengers with lower fares and new incentives, competing with each other for passengers.

Haute cuisine and haute couture

Buffet service in lounges, free champagne, roast beef carved on a cart at your seat, hot dogs for kids, inflight movies, and stereo sound competed for attention with stewardesses dressed in leotards and tunics designed by Emilio Pucci, miniskirts, lounging pajamas, sarongs, even hot pants. A myriad of choices faced the passenger. Alan Levy described the dilemma to *Life* readers in the October 29, 1965, issue:

"At 11 o'clock, Miss MacLaine implored me to make up my mind—red wine or champagne with my six-course TV lunch. I chose champagne because it promised to go well with the *Yellow Rose of Texas*. . . .There was a clatter of silverware as everyone switched jacks while Miss Starr served filet mignon. *Carry on Cabbie* was the umpteenth in a series of British B-pictures . . . in fluent Cockney, without English subtitles. When someone on my little screen said something I could swear was 'Red light means thruppence on the bloody clock,' I cut the movie sound and plugged into Stereo 2 and went on eating and watching. To the tune of *A Night on Bald Mountain*, *Carry on Cabbie* not only made sense, but seemed important."

Lower fares combined with the inflight entertainment to lure new passengers into the air. Families could fly for one-quarter to one-half the regular fare; passengers between the ages of 12 and 21 could travel on a half-fare, youth-standby basis, and a special "Discover America" promotion encouraged the growing vacation-travel market.

Personal travel credit cards provided "fly now, pay later" plans. Airlines also experimented with "no frills," one-class service and high-density seating on economy flights.

Coach travel, introduced in 1948, had already risen to 47 percent of the air travel market by 1960 and to 74 percent by 1963. Americans were after bargains. In 1958, the total number of air passengers went over the 50 million mark; in 1961, it topped 80 million, and it hit 100 million in 1965.

San Francisco to New York – 1967					
Plane	Cruising Speed	Number of Passengers	Time	Fare	Number of Stops
Boeing 707 or DC–8	550 m.p.h.	130	5 hours	First class $160 Coach $145	Nonstop

Services: Inflight movies, stereo, special meals for children, buffet service, cocktails, family fare, youth standby, Discover America fares

Total passengers carried by scheduled domestic airlines, 1967: 142,500,000

Faster than a jet plane

The standard airline joke in the 1960s was: "What takes twice as long as a jet plane to New York? The trip to the airport." It did not take passengers long to get used to speed in the air, and they expected the same swift service on the ground. Airlines introduced express baggage check-in, high-speed belts to move baggage more quickly, and huge baggage containers that were lifted onto the plane. Other innovations were more advanced computer reservation systems, moving sidewalks, closed-circuit television monitors that directed passengers to the proper gate, and inflight ticketing.

Congress authorized a program to build airports adequate for the jet age, but the airport dilemma had no easy solution. Jet planes required two-mile-long runways, and space was needed for future growth in passenger and cargo traffic. The first airport built expressly for the jet age, Dulles International, required an area two-thirds the size of Manhattan. Designed to eliminate the long walks of most large airports, Dulles used mobile lounges to carry passengers to the planes. Yet, the airport still suffers from the liability of being 27 miles from downtown Washington, D.C.

The flying commuter

A new kind of airline emerged in the postwar period to serve a new kind of air traveler, the business commuter, and to provide air service to smaller cities, which found themselves cut off from the nationwide air network when major airlines started leaping over them in the new long-range jets.

Commuter airlines grew rapidly, from 12 in 1965 to more than 160 in 1968. They carried more than 2 million passengers in 1968, operating from centrally located airfields and flying small planes—anything from sleek Beechcraft turboprop planes to Piper Aztecs to DC–3s, yes, even to the old Ford Trimotors. Island Airways flew tourists between Port Clinton, Ohio, and the Bass Islands in Lake Erie in the trusty Tin Goose.

Trunk airlines and local service carriers entered the commuter market too. In 1958, Allegheny began to offer low-fare, no-reservation commuter flights between Philadelphia and Pittsburgh. Tickets were sold during the flight, and commuters could buy ten-ticket discount books. Eastern Air Lines introduced the popular Washington–New York–Boston shuttle service. United Airlines, intrastate Pacific Southwest Airways, and Western Airlines served commuters between Los Angeles and San Francisco.

Helicopters and hovercraft joined the list of vehicles that tried to get more Americans to more places, more often, and more conveniently. The United States was a country on the go, and going faster all the time.

Television molded the view of the sixties—spacemen floating above the earth, Joe Namath gracefully rolling back for a pass, presidential candidates debating the issues, and, for insomniacs. . .heeerrre's Johnny!

Senator John F. Kennedy chatted with his rival for the presidency, Vice-President Richard M. Nixon, when they met by chance on a United Airlines plane in 1960.

Jets revolutionized air travel. They flew twice as high, twice as fast, and were twice as big as propeller planes. For the first time, no jet airport on earth was more than a day away from any other jet airport.

"It was unbelievable. All of a sudden, I could fly from New York to the West Coast for business and back the same night."

—Harry Thompson
salesman from New York City

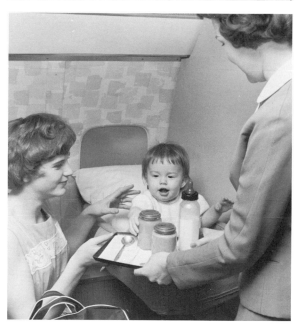

Families like Mr. and Mrs. Joseph Callahan and their ten children flying the new family plan fare helped to fill the big jets. Other discount fares of the 1960s—military and youth standbys and Discover America discounts—helped boost passenger totals by about 10 million people a year. In 1958, only about one-third of Americans had ever flown. By 1970, the percentage was nearing the halfway mark, and 50 percent of all travel was for pleasure.

One youth-fare standby recalled: "I was a college student and was really pinched for money. Spring vacation, a friend and I flew youth standby to Florida to visit my grandparents. The first flight had a jammed waiting room; we were sure we'd never get a seat, and had selfless arguments over who could be a martyr and stay behind if there were only one seat. It turned out there were 10 extras, and we flew out of there, feeling like bandits."

—Karen Moellen
nurse from Chicago

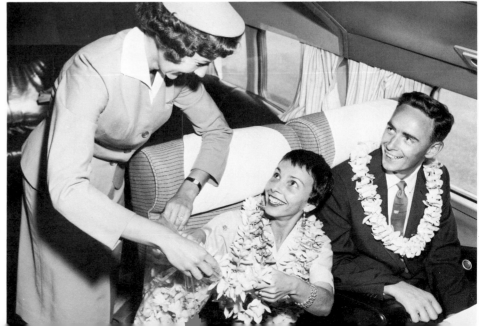

Innovative services attracted passengers during the 1960s. Continental Airlines featured a "Pink Buffet" service (lower left) with hors d'oeuvres, fruits, cheese, and complimentary champagne. Other airlines offered special food for children and served gourmet meals from carts.

Inflight movies were dubbed the "Great Escapo-Vision in the Sky" by *Life* writer Alan Levy, who reported: "I almost became the First Man Ever Lynched at 32,000 Feet—merely for lifting a shade to glimpse the Grand Canyon and thereby shedding unwanted light on a fluffy Technicolor marvel starring Sandra Dee. Boarding for my return a few days later on TWA's morning jet landing at Newark, I encountered some turbulence at the gate. Some of my fellow travelers had found out that our feature was Winston Churchill in 'The Finest Hours,' while, at the next gate, TWA's flight landing at Kennedy had immediate seating for one of the Rock Hudson vs. Doris Day epics. Mass defections from the Churchill flight followed."

In 1958, only 14 airports were ready to handle the jets, which required longer runways and larger terminals to accomodate the influx of passengers. Over the next few years, new airports were built in most major cities.

The new San Francisco airport and New York's John F. Kennedy International (formerly called Idlewild) introduced an innovative concept; a separate terminal was built for each airline. Individual airline terminals often were distinctive, like San Francisco's star-shaped United Airlines terminal (left) and TWA's graceful terminal at JFK (lower right), designed by Eero Saarinen.

Another innovation of the 1960s was a ramp leading from the second-story airport lounge to the doorway to the jet. The first ramps were open. Later, covered, telescoping "jetways" (top right) protected passengers from inclement weather.

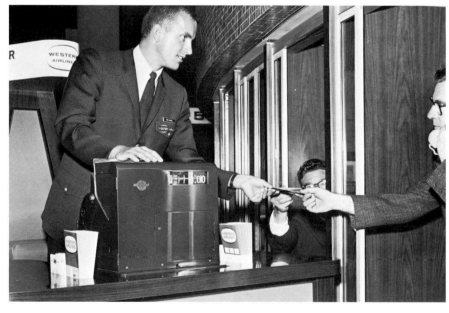

Revolving self-claim baggage carousels eased luggage retrieval, saving time for air travelers. Saving time was also the motivation for using helicopter service between airports and downtown and taking the new commuter flights, introduced in the 1960s. One innovative commuter line was Pacific Southwest Airways, whose primary route was Los Angeles–San Francisco, the most heavily traveled of all two-city markets in the world. Although PSA publicized its low fares and commuter schedules, most people noticed only the stewardesses.

The larger airlines also promoted commuter flights between large cities, with services like mobile ticket counters and inflight ticketing.

1968-1976

"**I** took one look, and I said to myself, Oh, nothing this big is going to fly. . ."

—Ginny Clausen
homemaker from San Francisco

But it flew, of course," Ginny Clausen sheepishly admitted, "and once I got used to it, I liked it a lot better. There was so much room to walk around and stretch out."

The wide-body, jumbo jets—the 747 in which Ginny Clausen flew, the DC–10 and the L1011—introduced a new era of airline travel. The most obvious difference, of course, was size. As a McDonnell Douglas industrial designer explained, the jumbo jets "gave us an interior more like a living room—a sort of flying baronial hall without a fireplace."

A fireplace was one of the few things the jumbo jets lacked. Passengers in the 1970s encountered magicians pulling rabbits out of hats, professional sport stars signing autographs, even Playboy bunnies, at 40,000 feet. When some people complained that flying had become boring now that planes flew above the weather, and often above the scenery, the airlines responded with entertainment. Everything from a piano bar in the lounge to feature-length movies, eight-channel stereo offering a choice of Bach or "Sesame Street," or talks by the editors of *Business Week*—even "live" broadcasts from the cockpit of the plane. If that did not work, travelers could eat and drink their way from coast to coast—with a champagne punch and buffet breakfast on an early morning flight to Hawaii, a deli sandwich and a beer for lunch, or free wine with your gourmet dinner of *entrecote mirabeau* or beef Wellington. One airline even moved its first-class diners to the upstairs lounge of the 747 and cooked meals to order—just like their favorite restaurants. Now people could go out to dinner on an airplane.

Some passengers were not so thrilled with the "show biz." "I'm like one of my hospital patients," said nurse Marian Schmitt. "I'd rather be left alone."

Well, with 370 passengers on one plane, there was bound to be many an idea for ways to spend the time, but there was also the room to cater to different tastes. As a consequence, airlines offered more options to passengers—smoking or non-smoking sections, earphones for those who wanted to listen to stereo entertainment, movies, or inflight magazines, and a choice of entrees at meals.

Computer, kosher and car rentals

Although not as visible as the giant jets, the computer brought about an even more profound revolution in air travel. Without the computer, it is doubtful that the airlines could have handled the enormous increase in passengers during the 1970s. In 1974, 45 million more passengers boarded commercial airplanes than had in 1968. Yet, thanks to computers, reservations, check-in, and other airport services now matched the speed of the flight itself. As one frequent traveler remarked, "Nowadays you get the feeling they know what they're doing; they're organized." The computer not only verified airline reservations in one quick phone call, but also printed the ticket and assigned a seat within seconds.

The computer also handled a number of other services for passengers—recording requests for special diets or wheelchairs to meet handicapped passengers. It traced lost suitcases by comparing the computer inventory of lost bags with the list of unclaimed bags. And, thanks to the computer, passengers could reserve rental cars and hotel rooms when they made their airline reservations.

The airlines offered complete travel packages, too. What is your pleasure—a long weekend scuba diving in the Caribbean, a family jaunt to Disneyland, a week at a tennis resort, two weeks at a dude ranch, a tour of the Hawaiian islands? Discount package tours helped make up for the loss of the youth fare, Discover America, and family fare

San Francisco to New York – 1976					
Plane	Cruising Speed	Number of Passengers	Time	Fare	Number of Stops
DC–10 or 747	550 m.p.h.	250–370	5 hours	First class $245 Coach $174	Nonstop

Services: Inflight movies and TV, stereo, live entertainment and electronic games, wide choice of meals, lounges, all-purpose discount fares, low-cost charter flights

Estimated total passengers carried by scheduled domestic airlines, 1976: 219,500,000

discounts, which were ruled discriminatory by the Civil Aeronautics Board and terminated in 1974. In 1975, airlines also offered a 25 percent discount of midweek flights of more than 750 miles. But the postwar rise in air travel flattened out during the 1970s. It rose briefly during the gasoline crisis, but slackened as the combination of recession and inflation pinched American pocketbooks.

And back on the ground

While jumbo jets coughed out 370 passengers at a time—and all their baggage—the airports of the 1960s tried to cope with the flood of travelers. An airport presented a fascinating panorama for the passenger who was not in a hurry, but it was often only an irritant to the harried business traveler like Boston passenger Harvey Cohn: "They're necessary. If you've seen one airport, you've seen them all. But they're just something you have to get through in order to get on a plane." In the 1970s, airlines and municipalities worked together to make it easier to use airports. In 1970, Congress authorized money for airport improvements and set up a trust fund similar to the Highway Trust Fund to provide monies for future development. The money was to be raised by passenger ticket and freight weigh-bill taxes. For existing airports came new, larger parking lots; more moving sidewalks; color-coded terminals with picture signs to help passengers find their way; rental luggage carts, and minibus shuttle service between parking lots and terminals.

Some cities established satellite airports throughout the metropolitan areas. New York for years has had LaGuardia and JFK, now handling about 6 million passengers a year, and Newark, handling another 3 million. By contrast, Chicago's O'Hare airport in the early 1970s handled 16 million passengers a year. Los Angeles diverted traffic from busy Los Angeles International by letting three satellite

airports in various suburbs handle the heavy commuter traffic to cities within a 500-mile radius. The main problem with this approach is finding the space for new airports and their long runways and providing transportation between airports for travelers with connecting flights. Helicopters, thought to be the answer in the 1960s, cost too much and carried too few passengers.

One solution may be the short takeoff and landing (STOL) airplanes, which can use downtown landing strips only 2,000 feet long. The STOLs may not only speed travel to and from the airports, but also may handle commuter traffic between downtown terminals, eliminating the drives to the airport.

Another answer has been the creation of airport cities that include hotels, convention facilities, and offices adjacent to terminals. Many traveling businessmen of the 1970s found they could transact their business without ever leaving the airport.

Undoubtedly, the major changes in air travel pending the arrival of supersonic aircraft will be improved methods of accomodating air travelers on the ground.

Americans on the move…a short hop by presidential helicopter…a voyage to the moon. And the boys from Liverpool flew in to look their fans over and became part of the American scene. "How did you find America?" the reporter asked. "Turned left at Greenland."

Jumbo crowds arrive for the jumbo jets. In 1975, over 207 million passengers boarded U.S. scheduled commercial airplanes, ten times more than in 1950.

"Every time I go to the airport, I say, 'Well, who're in all the cars?'"

—Janet Cary
secretary from Atlanta, Georgia

They're off on vacation, and he'll aways remember the day he earned his wings. His little sister will grow up taking air travel for granted, something many older Americans cannot do.

"I had my first plane trip when I was 45 years old. My little 10-year-old daughter took a trip to Cleveland from Chicago and she said, 'Oh, it was the most wonderful way to go.' And I said, this is silly. My little 10-year-old's not afraid to fly, so I took my first trip the next December. It was wonderful. I'm just sorry I waited so long."

—Edna Trass
homemaker from Gary, Indiana

Surging with people at midday, the
airport hubbub gradually subsides, until a
stewardess wearily heads home through
an empty corridor from the last flight of
the day. All day long, passengers come
and go, with all the paraphernalia that
comes with them—luggage, bicycles,
pets, wheelchairs, baby strollers,
backpacks, and briefcases.

"The best part is the speed...the part I
like least is waiting, waiting to get on,
waiting to make connections..."

—Harry Johnson
accountant from Milwaukee, Wisconsin

"I like to people-watch. Waiting at the
airport is one of the few times when I
really have free time just to sit down and
think and do what I want to do."

—Angela Cahn
bankteller from Denver, Colorado

Traveling with children is a challenge to the patience of any parent. "I get him some comic books and let him tear them up. I can't let him run up and down the aisle. I'd never see him again."

—Summer Avlonittis
homemaker from Idaho

Well, they know they'll eat again on the plane, but some have coffee and watch the planes take off and land, or grab a cup at the stand-up snack bar and check the morning headlines...or have just *one* of those hot fudge sundaes.

"I get up at the crack of dawn and nearly kill myself to get to the airport on time, and then I'm early, so I get a cup of coffe and a newspaper to kill a little time."

—George Kessler
insurance executive from New Orleans, Louisiana

"I don't use the airport restaurants. I'm too well fed on the plane."

—Jim Forest
student from Seattle, Washington

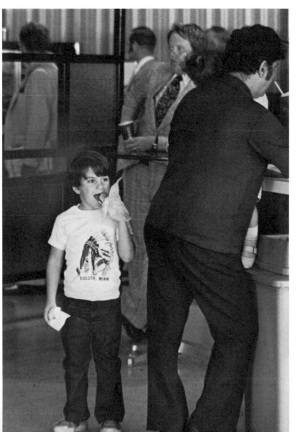

Check-in for smoking or non-smoking, window or aisle seat, and then line up to watch them load the baggage. Get a snapshot of the plane for your scrapbook.

"I love the anticipation…that you're going to meet new people and see new places."

—Sally Chapralis
writer from Chicago, Illinois

This traveling business can get a fellow mighty tired. But it is all worth it, when you meet grandma at the gate, and she wants to hear all about your trip. And, if it gets to be too much, you can always catch a nap at the airport.

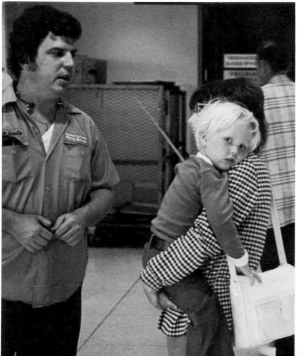

One passenger walked through the huge doorway from the passenger tunnel into the 747. She hesitated. "Where's the plane?" she asked, thinking she was still in an airport lounge.

There is plenty of room to walk around in the 747, with its 20-foot-wide cabin and 8-foot-high ceilings. Take several turns around the coach section and you have walked a quarter of a mile. Or lean back in your seat in the DC-10 wide-body jet and enjoy television—regular programs while the airplane is on the ground and closed-circuit features while aloft.

"I like to see the pilots, size 'em up before I get on the plane. Today before I left I was eating breakfast in the airport coffee shop...one group of pilots came in and sat down. They looked real competent, you know, dressed real sharp and everything. I told the person who brought me to the airport, 'I hope that's my pilot there.'"

—Ann Samsell
veterinarian from West Virginia

103

It is a big plane, and there is something for everyone—a chance to relax in the lounge with a friend…a chance to talk to a pro athlete…a hot pastrami sandwich and cold beer instead of a full luncheon…or a chance to have a cocktail and finish the novel you thought you would have time to read on vacation.

"Coming back from the West Coast, it was a champagne flight…we had a wonderful meal, the stewardess was very friendly. It was a good time, nice conversation, a very memorable experience. You don't get that on a short flight. It's just bam, and you're there and gone."

—Edward Nesteruk
businessman from Columbus, Ohio

"I read magazines and write…I try to talk to the people next to me. I enjoy meeting people, and I usually try to strike up a conversation. I've met some really interesting people."

—Carrie Nielsen
social worker from Minneapolis, Minnesota

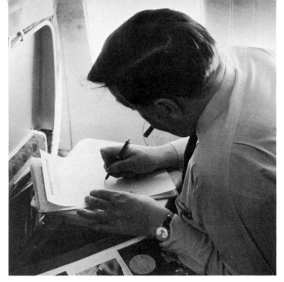

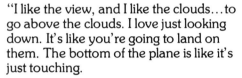

"I like the view, and I like the clouds…to go above the clouds. I love just looking down. It's like you're going to land on them. The bottom of the plane is like it's just touching.

"And if I'm near the wing, I always look at the wing and how that rudder, whatever it is, moves up and down.

"And I like the things on planes…it's just fun sitting in the plane. My enjoyment of it is just looking out the window. And I bring art papers and stuff like that and draw and loosen my seat belt and pretend I'm an astronaut sometimes; I try to get up out of my seat and float around.

"I've always wanted to see a movie on an airline…I did listen to their headset and I liked that a lot. And I heard, once in a great while, I heard "Sesame Street" over it, and I wish they'd put that back on."

—Eric John Matthies
seven-year-old child from Chicago

"After a while it becomes a way to get around. You take it for granted. I never look out the window. I work or read. It's off the plane, grab the bag, get the car, and off to an appointment."

—John Hedry
executive from Detroit, Michigan

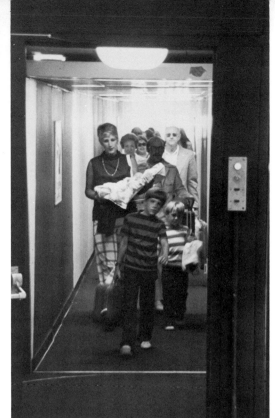

Endings…a letdown because the trip is over…arms loaded with souvenirs and gifts for the folks back home…a lonely bus ride into a new city and an unfamiliar hotel…waiting for your ride…loading your golf clubs and bags into the trunk. For some, the end of a memorable experience; for a few, just another day, another flight, another town.

And for others, a warm welcome and the best part of all, getting together with those you love.

108

Epilogue

From open cockpit planes to jumbo jets…few pioneer airline passengers could have forecast what the first fifty years of commercial air travel would bring. And the armchair experts of today will probably fall short in their predictions for the next 50 years. Already, intercontinental commercial space flights are being discussed by aeronautical engineers. The magic sails of the future? We will just have to wait and see.

Acknowledgments

United Airlines and Graphic Alliance are grateful to the following individuals, companies and institutions for their valuable assistance in making available documentary materials and photographs in their collections:

Air Transport Association of America: *Linda Kloster*

American Airlines: *David C. Frailey*

American Hall of Aviation History: *David D. Hatfield*

The Bettmann Archive, Inc.

The Boeing Company: *Harl Brackin*

Continental Airlines: *Joseph A. Daley, John Clayton*

Delta Air Lines: *Harriet Parker*

Eastern Air Lines: *Robert V. Christian*

Ford Archives: *David Crippen*

McDonnell Douglas Corporation: *Ray Towne, Harry Calkins, H.S. Gann*

Mr. and Mrs. Ralph Morgan, Denver, Colorado

Northwest Orient Airlines: *Walter T. Hellman*

Pacific Southwest Airlines: *Terry Henry*

Pan American World Airways: *Antonio Lutz, Ann Whyte*

Franklin Delano Roosevelt Library: *William Emerson*

Smithsonian Institution, National Air and Space Museum: *Catherine Scott*

Trans World Airlines: *Barry F. Wiksten, Rose Scotti, J.W. Cosley*

United Press International

Western Air Lines: *Ray Silvius, Linda Cole*

We thank the following individuals who allowed the author to interview them: Summer Avlonittis; Ted Bennett; Angela Cahn; Maude Campbell; Janet Cary; Ken Case; Sally Chapralis; Ginny Clausen; Harvey Cohn; Fred Daniels; Jim Forest; John Hedry; Tom Jamison; Harvey Johnson; George Kessler; Ralph Martin; Eric John Matthies; Karen Moellen; Carrie Neilson; Edward Nesteruk; Ann Samsell; Marian Schmitt; Harry Thompson; Edna Trass.

We wish to thank the following publishers for permission to reprint excerpts from their works:

Will Rogers, "Flying and Eating My Way East," *The Saturday Evening Post*, January 21, 1928. Reprinted with permission from *The Saturday Evening Post*, © 1928 The Curtis Publishing Company and with permission of Will Rogers, Jr.

J.C. Furnas, "Mr. Milquetoast in the Sky," *Scribners*, September, 1938

Douglas J. Ingells, *The Plane That Changed The World, A Biography of the DC-3*, Fallbrook, California, Aero Publisher, Inc. 1966

"High Drinks," *The New Yorker*, October 7, 1950

Robert J. Serling, "When Western Went To War" *Western's World Magazine*, Summer, 1975

Don Eddy, "Bumped Off," *The American Magazine*, February, 1945

"What's Wrong With the Airlines," *Fortune* Magazine, August, 1946

"Leavin' on a Jet Plane" by John Denver, Copyright © 1967—Cherry Lane Music Co. Used by Permission—All Rights Reserved.

Alan Levy, "The Great Escapo-Vision in the Sky," *Life* Magazine, October 29, 1965, Copyright © 1965 by Time Inc. Reprinted with permission.

Sources/Photographs

We are grateful to the following individuals, companies, and institutions for giving us permission to reproduce photographs from their collections. Credits for each page are listed clockwise from top left corner.

Part I

P. 4—Ralph Morgan
P. 5—United Press International, Bettmann Archive, United Airlines, Bettmann
P. 6—Smithsonian Institution, National Air and Space Museum; David D. Hatfield
P. 7—United Airlines
P. 8—Smithsonian
P. 9—United
P. 10—United
P. 11—United
P. 12—Smithsonian
P. 13—Western Airlines
P. 14—Hatfield, Western, Smithsonian
P. 15—United
P. 16—United
P. 17—Ford Archives, Dearborn, Michigan; Ford Archives; Smithsonian; Ford Archives

P. 18—Air Transport Association of America, Pan American World Airways, The Boeing Company, Eastern Air Lines
P. 19—United
P. 20—Ralph Morgan
P. 21—Ralph Morgan, United, Ralph Morgan
P. 22—Western, United, United
P. 23—United
P. 24—United
P. 25—Boeing, Western, Western, Western
P. 26—Trans World Airlines, Smithsonian, Smithsonian
P. 27—Smithsonian
P. 28—Western
P. 29—Northwest Orient Airlines
P. 30—United
P. 31—Boeing, United, United, United

Part II

P. 36—Bettmann
P. 37—Ralph Morgan, American Airlines, Franklin D. Roosevelt Library
P. 38—Ralph Morgan
P. 39—Boeing

P. 40—United, United, United, Morgan
P. 41—United, Western
P. 42—United
P. 43—Delta Air Lines, Morgan, United
P. 44—United
P. 45—Morgan, United, McDonnell Douglas Corporation
P. 46—United, United, Western
P. 47—United, United, Morgan
P. 48—Smithsonian
P. 49—Morgan, Smithsonian, Bettmann, Smithsonian
P. 50—Pan American, Pan American, Pan American, Boeing
P. 51—Pan American

Part III

P. 56—UPI, Bettmann, UPI
P. 57—UPI
P. 58—TWA, TWA, TWA, Delta, United
P. 59—TWA
P. 60—Western
P. 61—Northwest, United, United
P. 62—UPI, United, United, United, United

P. 63—United
P. 64—TWA
P. 65—Pan Am, United, Western, United
P. 66—Smithsonian, Morgan
P. 67—United
P. 68—United, Pan American, Boeing, Pan American, Pan American
P. 69—Boeing
P. 70—United
P. 71—TWA, United, United, TWA

Part IV

P. 76—Bettmann, UPI
P. 77—UPI, United
P. 78—United
P. 79—Pan American
P. 80—Western, Western, United, Delta
P. 81—United
P. 82—United, Continental Airlines, Continental
P. 83—United
P. 84—United
P. 85—United, Pan American, Western, TWA
P. 86—United, Boeing, Pacific Southwest Airways, Western
P. 87—Western

Part V

P. 92—Bettmann
P. 93—UPI
P. 94–102—United
P. 103—United, TWA
P. 104—United
P. 105—United, United, Western, Boeing
P. 106—Boeing
P. 107—United, Western, United
P. 108—United
P. 190—United

DAILY AIR
SCHEDULE

PAN AMERICAN
AIRWAYS SYSTEM

AMERICA'S INTERNATIONAL
AIR TRANSPORT SYSTEM

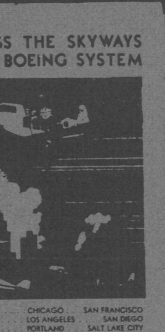

ACROSS THE SKYWAYS
WITH BOEING SYSTEM

NEW YORK	CHICAGO	SAN FRANCISCO
SEATTLE	LOS ANGELES	SAN DIEGO
SEATTLE	PORTLAND	SALT LAKE CITY

EFFECTIVE OCTOBER 1, 1933

UNITED
AIR LINES

Fly This Winter
in Heated, Comfortable Cabin Planes

LOW FARES
To 157 Cities in 38 States

Air Transportation at Its

UNITED AIR

SUBSIDIARY OF UNITED AIRCRAFT & TRANS

UNITED AIR LINES
TRANSPORT CORPORATION

VIA AIR

UNIT
AIR LI

AIR LOG
OF A FLIGHT WITH
UNITED AIR LI

MOHAWK AIRLINES
The Route of the Aircraft

UNITED AIR LINES
VARNEY AIR LINES DIVISION

2½ Hrs.

SAN FRANCISCO - LOS ANGELES

UNITED AIR LINES announce the only direct non-stop passenger plane service from
San Francisco Peninsula to Los Angeles and San Diego

2 PLANES DAILY

$18.95 $27.95

UNITED AIR LINES

TRAVEL BY AIR

WESTERN
AIR
Express
National Parks Route

SEATTLE, TACOMA, PORTLAND, MEDFORD,
SAN FRANCISCO, OAKLAND, LOS ANGELES,
SAN DIEGO

Pacific Air Transport Subsidiary

United Air Lines

New BORDER TO BORDER
AIR TRANSPORT SERVICE Da Luce
ALL-DAYLIGHT

PAC

TEXAS

Now you c
DALLAS
MONR
BIR

Daily Service
SAFE • SWIFT

DELT